My Little BIT OF GRIT

PETER PAUPER PRESS, INC.
Rye Brook, New York

PETER PAUPER PRESS

In 1928, at the age of twenty-two, Peter Beilenson began printing books on a small press in the basement of his parents' home in Larchmont, New York. Peter—and later, his wife, Edna—sought to create fine books that sold at "prices even a pauper could afford."

Today, still family owned and operated, Peter Pauper Press continues to honor our founders' legacy of quality, value, and fun for big kids and small kids alike.

Written by Hannah Beilenson
Designed by Heather Zschock

3 International Drive
Rye Brook, NY 10573 USA

Published in the UK and Europe by Peter Pauper Press, Inc.
c/o White Pebble International
Units 2-3, Spring Business Park
Stanbridge Road
Havant, Hampshire PO9 2GJ, UK

ISBN 978-1-4413-4209-6
Printed in China

7 6 5 4 3 2 1

OUR ACTIONS AND US

Have you ever tried something new? Shared a toy or snack? Given a hug or high five when someone needed it? Well, those are just a few examples of putting your feelings into action! And every action you take can make a change. You can make people smile and laugh, help others feel safe, and create something new for everyone to share. There's so much you can do, and there's no wrong place to start—so let's take action today!

One action is **Grit**, and we'll meet someone who will help us learn more about it.

This math homework is too hard.

It'll take forever to clean my room.

I can't get this painting right.
That's it! I give up.

Don't give up yet! You can do it.
Who said that?

Down here!
What are you?
I'm a **Bit of Grit**.

Grit? What's that?
Grit is when you keep trying despite any challenges you might face.

It means you don't give up just because something is hard. It's when you persevere.

Just because it feels impossible doesn't mean it is. It just means you have to think about it in a different way.

You can get creative

or ask for help.
HELP
ME!
(For a free cookie!)

You can practice and come back to it later.

You can take deep breaths and try again.

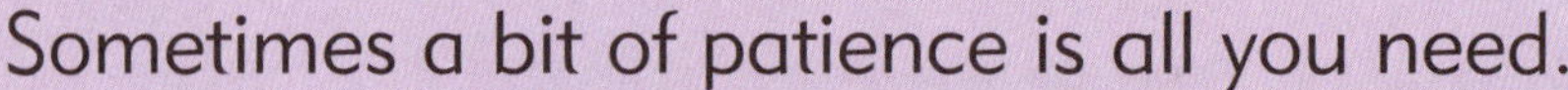

I guess that's true. But what's the point? It's not fun when things are so hard.

It's not always fun, but perseverance is still important.

It helps you learn,

it can lead to good things,

and it lets you connect
with other people.

You don't have to figure it out all by yourself.
Everyone has a hard time now and then.

Yeah, everyone needs a
bit of grit sometimes.
And listening to how other
people face challenges can
make facing your own
a little easier.

Now that we've talked about it, I think I feel better.
That's great. Are you ready to try again?
Definitely!

Meet My Bit of Grit

My Bit of Grit's name is:

....

When things are tough, I can:

....

....

....

Grit helps me because:

....

....

....

....